STRESS MANAGEMENT BLUEPRINT

STRESS MANAGEMENT BLUEPRINT

Practical Strategies for Resilience and Inner Peace

INNER POWER

Inner Strength Counselling

CONTENTS

CHAPTER 1

Introduction

In today's fast-paced world, stress seems like an unwelcome guest in almost everyone's life. The burden of pressure triggers anxiety, leaving many of us feeling unprepared and overwhelmed. These feelings of anxiety not only affect our mental well-being but can also take a toll on our physical health.

Consider this: one in every eight Americans aged 18-54 battles an anxiety disorder, totaling over 19 million people! Astonishingly, anxiety disorders top the charts as the leading mental health concern among American women, only trailing behind alcohol and drug abuse among men.

Statistics reveal a stark reality: women endure stress and anxiety nearly twice as much as men. Anxiety disorders surpass even depression, making them the most prevalent mental illness in America. Surprisingly, anxiety isn't exclusive to the young; it's the most common mental health issue faced by adults over 65. The yearly expenses associated with anxiety disorders in the United States. hits a staggering $46.6 billion, and those affected visit an average of five doctors before getting a successful diagnosis.

Stress and anxiety are inseparable companions. Stress, responsible for 80% of all illnesses, often manifests itself in the form of anxiety. However, its detrimental effects reach far beyond what we may realize. Recent findings indicate that stress can significantly impact our health in ways previously underestimated.

Reports from Health Psychology magazine highlight that chronic stress disrupts the body's immune system, leaving individuals more susceptible to various illnesses, from allergies to cardiovascular diseases. During prolonged periods of stress, non-essential bodily functions, like the immune and digestive systems, shut down, making us more vulnerable to sickness.

Moreover, stress often triggers unhealthy behaviors like smoking, excessive drinking, poor dietary habits, or a lack of physical activity, further compromising our health. It's evident: stress isn't just the strain we feel—it's a catalyst for a cascade of health issues.

Yet, stress is an inevitable part of life. What truly matters is our response to it. While eliminating stress entirely might seem impossible, learning effective coping mechanisms can transform stress into a manageable force.

When I was tasked with writing this book, I initially contemplated extreme solutions to banish stress and anxiety entirely. However, isolating oneself isn't the answer. I've battled anxiety disorders stemming from stress for years, and through my experiences and insights from experts, I've compiled practical tools to help navigate stressful situations.

This book aims to share invaluable advice on combating debilitating anxiety and panic attacks. Throughout my research, I've stumbled upon eye-opening information that I'm excited to impart. Join me on this journey to discover ways to eliminate stress and anxiety from your life!

CHAPTER 2

Rediscovering Control

In these challenging times, life often feels like an uphill battle, filled with pain and unfairness. Despite these struggles, we persevere, hoping and praying for brighter days. However, the world seems to be growing increasingly chaotic and uncertain, making it a stressful place to live. Safety feels like an illusion, debts skyrocket, jobs vanish, and the overall well-being of many hangs by a thread. For far too many, worry, depression, and anxiety have become a constant companion.

Welcome to the Age of Anxiety. Time magazine's cover boldly declared it in 2002, reflecting the pervasive anxiety of living in the 21st century. The continuous stress of our modern world has taken its toll, leaving many trapped in a cycle of fear and worry.

The tragedy of September 11 amplified this constant anxiety. Even today, four years later, the haunting fear of a similar catastrophe persists in the minds of many, lingering like an unwelcome shadow.

Every news channel and newspaper bombards us with distressing images and stories, making us question our safety at every turn. In this digital era, information inundates us like never before, overwhelming our senses.

Economic woes add to the strain. Rising gas prices, exorbitant housing costs, and soaring food prices force many into unfulfilling jobs just to make ends meet. The pursuit of a dream career takes a backseat to the necessity of a paycheck.

The influx of women in the workforce adds another layer of stress. Balancing multiple roles—earner, homemaker, parent, spouse—leaves many women neglecting self-care, contributing to soaring stress levels.

Even children aren't exempt from stress. Teens, aspiring for higher education, find themselves juggling intense studies for scholarships amidst skyrocketing tuition fees. Part-time jobs become essential to afford what their parents can't, adding to the pressure cooker of peer expectations.

In a world dominated by cell phones, the internet, and constant connectivity, we've forgotten to pause and savor life. We've succumbed to the pressure of perpetual motion, forgetting that it's okay to slow down and enjoy life's simple pleasures.

The compulsion to keep up with this whirlwind stems from a sense of obligation rather than genuine desire. The inability to say "No" piles up unnecessary expectations and obligations, fueling our anxiety.

Stress and anxiety are common facets of life. It's only when they seize control of our lives that they transform into problems.

Each of us encounters situations causing stress and anxiety – whether it's buying property, hosting guests, academic pressures, financial strains, or relationship issues. Stress becomes overwhelming when we feel powerless in these circumstances.

But here's the uplifting truth: you possess the power within to overcome stress and anxiety. Often, we overlook this power amidst the chaos. The tools are within your grasp; it's time to wield them.

Let's start by dismantling the barriers hindering our path to a healthier, stress-free life.

CHAPTER 3

Overcoming Stress-Induced Behaviors

In the pursuit of a stress-free life, recognizing and addressing certain behaviors can significantly impact your healing journey. These behaviors often act as barriers, hindering progress towards a more serene existence.

Firstly, there's obsessive negativity. This tendency involves a constant "negative" outlook toward people, situations, or life itself. Phrases like "I can't do this!" or "Nothing ever works!" might frequently escape your lips. This "sour grapes" attitude limits your ability to see life's positives and hampers your appreciation for the beauty within and around you.

Next, obsessive perfectionism takes center stage. It involves an obsession with doing everything "just right," often leading to overwhelming anxiety. Statements like "I must do this perfectly!" or "I'll be a failure if I'm not precise!" highlight this behavior. Such tendencies rob you of the ability to enjoy life without feeling constantly stressed.

Lastly, there's obsessive analysis. This behavior involves incessantly revisiting tasks or issues, believing that repeated scrutiny is essential. Statements like "I need to study this inside-out!" or "Overthinking prevents things from going wrong!" exemplify this trait. While analytical thinking is valuable, excessive analysis robs you of moments to savor life's experiences.

Identifying and understanding these "Blocking Behaviors" is pivotal to releasing stress and regaining control over anxiety.

If you suspect engaging in these behaviors, seeking input from trusted individuals can be enlightening. Asking loved ones for honest feedback—such as, "Am I negative or complain frequently?"—may be uncomfortable but offers valuable insights into how others perceive you. Embrace their feedback as constructive, providing invaluable self-awareness.

Moreover, maintaining a journal to note instances of these behaviors can be enlightening. Even if writing isn't your forte, jotting down daily entries reveals behavioral patterns that hinder progress in managing anxiety.

This book will later provide effective stress-relief techniques. However, recognizing these barriers is the crucial initial step toward healing and conquering stress and anxiety.

Many confuse stress with anxiety, assuming they're synonymous. However, they're distinct experiences with their characteristics and impacts.

CHAPTER 4

Decoding Stress, Anxiety, and Their Impact

Contrary to common belief, stress and anxiety are distinct experiences. Stress arises from life's pressures, activating our bodies with adrenaline due to work or other demanding tasks. Prolonged exposure to stress hormones may lead to depression, elevated blood pressure, and other adverse effects.

Anxiety, on the other hand, is a state where fear overwhelms emotions, accompanied by worry and apprehension. It can manifest as isolation and intense nervousness, accompanied by physical symptoms like chest pains, dizziness, shortness of breath, and panic attacks.

Stress originates from specific stressors, while anxiety persists even after the stressor vanishes. What's stressful for one person might not affect another similarly. Anxiety, often accompanied by a sense of impending doom, can arise without a recognized source, intensifying distress.

Our bodies and minds react to stress by disrupting life's balance, triggered by fear or threats. Adrenaline release during stressful events causes increased heart rate, elevated blood pressure, muscle tension, and dilated pupils. Yet, not all stress elicits extreme reactions; responses vary, and not every stressful situation induces extreme duress.

Individual susceptibility to stress differs. Everyday decisions might seem overwhelming for some, while others thrive under pressure, becoming highly productive.

Women with children tend to have higher stress hormone levels, but this doesn't negate the stress experiences of women without children. It's essential for mothers to allocate self-care time, reducing stress for better parenting and managing daily challenges.

Anxiety, a feeling of unease, is common in stressful situations, like exams or illness. It can be a useful experience but becomes problematic when excessive or prolonged. Anxiety disorders often accompany other psychiatric conditions, such as depression, impacting daily activities.

The physical symptoms of anxiety, triggered by the brain's "fight or flight" response, include diarrhea, dry mouth, rapid heartbeat, insomnia, irritability, difficulty concentrating, and feelings of unreality.

Anxiety can arise from stress, excessive worry, drug side effects or withdrawal, poor diet, performance pressures, PTSD, adrenal gland tumors, or other factors. Excessive anxiety and stress may lead to depression, a manageable condition with proper care.

Let's now explore quizzes to determine if you're experiencing high stress, excessive anxiety, or depression.

CHAPTER 5

Understanding Stress & Anxiety

Before delving into this, it's important to clarify that we're not medical professionals. This information, drawn from reliable sources, isn't intended for diagnosis but rather as a guide to help recognize and address potential issues effectively.

Let's start by understanding depression, which can be more than occasional blues. Clinical depression exhibits symptoms over a prolonged period, impacting life significantly. Answer the following questions, considering consistent feelings over two weeks:

1. Do you feel persistently sad?
2. Are simple tasks like showering or cooking challenging due to lack of motivation?
3. Have others noticed you being overly irritable?

4. Do you struggle with concentration?
5. Do you feel isolated even around family and friends?
6. Have your interests waned?
7. Do you feel hopeless or worthless without reason?
8. Are you constantly tired of sleep troubles?
9. Has your weight fluctuated significantly?

Answering "Yes" to five or more questions could indicate clinical depression, warranting professional help. Seeking support was transformative for me; it could be for you too!

Moving on to stress:

1. Do constant worries and negative self-talk plague your mind?
2. Does concentration become difficult?
3. Are anger and impulsive reactions common?
4. Do recurring headaches or neck pain trouble you?
5. Are you grinding your teeth?
6. Does overwhelming anxiety or depression often strike?
7. Do you indulge in unhealthy habits to cope?
8. Do small joys fail to satisfy?
9. Do minor issues provoke disproportionate anger?

Answering "Yes" to most suggests high stress levels. Fortunately, this book will equip you with valuable coping techniques.

Now, about anxiety:

1. Do you experience breathlessness, palpitations, or shaking at rest?
2. Is there a fear of losing control or going crazy?
3. Do social situations induce fear, leading to avoidance?
4. Are specific objects sources of fear?
5. Do you fear being trapped in certain situations?
6. Is leaving your home a source of fear?
7. Do persistent intrusive thoughts plague you?
8. Do you feel compelled to repeat activities?
9. Do distressing past events recur persistently?

Answering "Yes" to more than four indicates potential anxiety disorder.

Depression, excessive stress, or anxiety aren't trivial concerns. They demand attention to safeguard overall health.

Stress and anxiety impact various bodily functions. Managing these involves discipline and maintaining a proper schedule. Recognize your limits and avoid overexertion, taking small steps forward.

Remember, stress is natural but unchecked can lead to physical, emotional, and behavioral disorders, impacting health and relationships.

Panic attacks, a severe outcome of stress and anxiety, demand exploration. Let's delve deeper into this subject.

CHAPTER 6

Panic Attacks

Experiencing excessive stress and anxiety can trigger intense physical responses, leading to panic attacks. I vividly recall my first panic attack during a drive home from a football game—it was anything but restful. Feeling disconnected, struggling to breathe, and racing heart—it was like my body was betraying me. Pulling over on the highway, I hoped to walk it off but couldn't catch my breath. It felt like a terrifying ordeal, though, obviously, I wasn't dying.

Since then, I've encountered many panic attacks but learned to recognize and manage them. Let's explore the signs that indicate a looming panic attack:

- Palpitations
- Rapid heart rate
- Sweating
- Trembling or shaking

- Shortness of breath
- Feeling choked
- Chest discomfort
- Nausea or stomach cramps
- Derealization (feeling detached from reality)
- Fear of losing control or dying
- Numbness or tingling in limbs
- Chills or hot flashes

The intensity of panic attacks often leads people to the emergency room, mistaking them for heart attacks. Explaining this to loved ones can be challenging; their impatience or disbelief can compound the distress.

Imagine waiting in a grocery store line, feeling discomfort rise—tightness in your chest, breathlessness, and palpitations. You scan the environment, feeling a surge of panic, knowing an attack is imminent. Trying breathing exercises, focusing on relaxing thoughts—all in vain. The anxiety heightens, and you're left feeling helpless, considering an abrupt exit.

If you've experienced panic attacks, this scenario may resonate deeply. The triggers and sensations might vary, but the reality of panic attacks is undeniable.

I recall an incident at home, seemingly safe when panic struck suddenly. No apparent stressors, just overwhelming symptoms. Stepping outside for fresh air and deep breathing helped, but it left me puzzled—why did it happen without any warning?

That's the enigma of panic—your mind can play tricks, triggering attacks unexpectedly. Despite the uncertainty, there are coping mechanisms to combat panic attacks and navigate these situations more effectively.

CHAPTER 7

Coping Strategies for Panic Attacks

Coping with anxiety disorders can vary greatly, yet recognizing the onset of a panic attack is crucial. Those frequently experiencing panic attacks might develop acute anxiety disorders, at times confining them to their homes.

Understanding the sensations preceding a panic attack is key. Many struggle to grasp the feeling of disconnection—an unsettling state where physical objects are perceived but doubted. It's akin to being a spectator in your own life, devoid of control, an utterly distressing experience.

Curiously, combating panic attacks begins with the willingness to confront them. The paradoxical trick lies in not fearing these attacks. The more you dread them, the more likely they'll surface. It's about challenging and standing up to them, reducing their grip.

Imagine standing on a cliff's edge; anxiety pushes you closer to falling over. To overcome it, metaphorically 'jump' into the fear, welcoming it rather than resisting.

An important fact: panic attacks won't cause harm, though the sensations may feel extreme. The 'jump' becomes nothing more than a two-foot drop—perfectly safe.

Anxiety disrupts life's balance, shifting focus from the body's center to overwhelming mental worry. To counter panic attacks, focus on relaxation. Concentrating on slow, steady breathing helps regulate your heart rate and quell panic.

A helpful breathing technique involves emptying your lungs completely, prompting deeper breaths afterward. Pressing your feet against the ground or a wall while breathing deeply can ground you and alleviate panic.

Utilize your senses to stay present—observe surroundings, touch, sound, smell, or even call a friend. Aromatherapy with oils like lavender, helichrysum, frankincense, or marjoram might offer calming effects. Preparing positive affirmations and coping strategies in advance can aid during panic episodes.

Visualization techniques can also be beneficial. Visualize peaceful scenarios or calming landscapes to redirect focus away from panic.

CHAPTER 8

Visualization Techniques for Reducing Anxiety and Stress

Visualization serves as a potent method to alleviate mental stress and tension, especially during anxious episodes. This exercise, when practiced regularly for longer durations, effectively eliminates deep-seated anxieties or intrusive thoughts.

There exists no strict method for visualization; follow your intuition without feeling pressured to create clear mental images. Initially performed in a quiet space, the practice gradually becomes adaptable to busier environments, fostering a sense of mental release and relaxation.

To commence, whether seated or standing, shut your eyes and focus on your breath. Pay attention to your breath's rhythm and practice Diaphragmatic Breathing—wherein your stomach expands while breathing in and gently falls back during exhalation.

After mastering this technique, attempt to slow your breathing pace further by introducing a pause after exhaling and before inhaling again. Establishing a rhythm—such as counting to three during inhalation and exhalation—helps maintain focus, minimizing intrusive thoughts.

Should distracting thoughts arise, acknowledge them and return your focus to breathing and counting. This practice, when consistently performed, not only aids relaxation but also strengthens the Diaphragmatic Muscle, fostering a constant relaxed state.

Direct your attention to your feet, attempting to genuinely sense each toe. Envision roots extending from your soles into the earth, firmly anchoring you like a sturdy tree. Embrace this sensation of stability and safety.

Now, visualize a radiant cloud forming above, followed by a bolt of light igniting at your crown. As this luminous band descends slowly through your body, imagine it clearing your mind of stressful or distressing thoughts. Repeat this imagery several times until a sense of clearing and release pervades your being.

Conclude by picturing yourself under a vibrant, revitalizing waterfall. Feel the water cascading over you, refreshing every inch of your body. Engage your senses—taste the water, listen to its melody, and feel its rejuvenating touch.

Employing all senses in visualization enhances its efficacy. By making these mental images vivid and lifelike, using touch, taste, and sound, the benefits intensify. Regular practice allows the mind to relinquish accumulated stress, much like a muscle that needs to unwind regularly.

Create mental landscapes or scenarios that induce calmness—a 'happy place' like a serene beach or a comforting setting. These visualizations signal the brain to release accumulated tension and anxious thoughts.

Consistent daily practice is key to mastering stress release. Initiate this routine before bedtime to promote sound sleep. Visualization isn't limited to the bedroom; some prefer a dedicated space to concentrate solely on mental imagery.

While visualization may not terminate anxiety attacks, it can effectively prevent their onset. Over time, it significantly diminishes general anxiety levels, granting days free from intrusive thoughts and fostering inner calm.

Visualization stands as an effective tool to counter anxious thoughts. Let's explore other techniques to combat excessive stress, beginning with the influence of music.

CHAPTER 9

Harnessing the Soothing Power of Music

Music is a potent tool for stress alleviation, but its effectiveness varies with individual tastes. Choosing music that resonates positively is crucial, as forced exposure to relaxation tunes one dislikes may induce stress rather than alleviate it. Music holds significant sway over our moods and acts as a stress reliever on multiple levels.

The human energy system responds uniquely to sounds, with distinct tones and frequencies influencing the body and chakra centers. Engaging in music creation or playing instruments can yield positive effects beyond listening.

Upon hearing music, a surge in deep breathing is among the initial stress-relief responses. Moreover, the body accelerates serotonin production. Background music in workplaces has shown remarkable stress reduction effects, akin to how retail places use it to distract shoppers from high prices.

Studies reveal that music reduces heart rates and induces relaxation, particularly when coupled with relaxation therapy. Experts attribute this calming effect to music's rhythm or beat, echoing the soothing influence of a mother's heartbeat in infancy, fostering a sense of security and relaxation.

However, not all music has the same calming effect. Surprisingly, certain Celtic, Native American, and percussion-based tunes have proven exceptionally soothing, contrasting with some traditional meditation and relaxation recordings that exhibited adverse EEG patterns.

Personal preference plays a vital role in selecting music. What works for one person may not benefit another. Opt for music that resonates positively, such as serene ocean sounds paired with piano melodies from a rest and relaxation CD.

Be mindful of avoiding music associated with past sad memories while trying to de-stress. Focus on music that encourages relaxation and peace rather than inducing unwanted emotions.

Here are some pointers for leveraging music to de-stress effectively:

- Delve into a 20-minute "sound bath" by lying comfortably near speakers or wearing headphones, listening to slow-paced, cyclical music, focusing on breathing, and allowing stress to dissipate.

- For a burst of energy after work, opt for faster music and dance along, leveraging music's stimulation for stress release.

- Rely on familiar tunes like childhood favorites or oldies for a calming effect during tough times.

- Combine music with a brisk walk, syncing breathing with the rhythm, or listen to nature sounds like ocean waves or forest ambiance for a calming effect.

Aside from music, self-hypnosis is another effective relaxation technique for managing anxiety issues.

CHAPTER 10

The Practice of Self-Hypnosis

Amidst overwhelming stress and anxiety, I found myself teetering on the brink, where everything seemed to spiral out of control. Engaged in writing about yoga and meditation, I chanced upon a website offering a downloadable audio session for hypnotic relaxation. The small investment turned out to be an invaluable reprieve.

Numerous online platforms offer these sessions for a small fee, but the practice of self-hypnosis independently is entirely feasible. It begins by discovering a serene space where the mind can genuinely relax and listen to its inner voice. Embracing the process naturally, without forcing any outcome, allows the hypnotic state to evolve organically. Actively searching for specific signs or signals indicating the hypnotic state impedes relaxation and the benefits of self-hypnosis.

Each individual's experience with hypnosis is unique, yet universally offers a pleasant state without any adverse effects. Self-hypnosis is a skill that improves over time, gaining potency with practice.

Setting up a consistent practice schedule, dedicating 10 to 30 minutes depending on availability, enhances the experience. Optimal practice times, when interruptions are least likely, significantly contribute to its effectiveness. Many find lying down in a comfortable, distraction-free environment ideal for practice. In case of disruptive noise, consider using background sounds like stereo music or white noise—easily mimicked by tuning a radio receiver between stations.

The fundamental phases of a hypnotic induction encompass relaxation, deepening, suggestion application, and termination. Begin with relaxation, gradually easing tensions using techniques like Jacobson Progressive Relaxation. Deepening procedures transition from relaxation to a deeper hypnotic state, emphasizing the importance of allowing this transition to occur naturally.

The suggestion application phase involves tailored affirmations or pre-prepared statements, focusing on desired outcomes. Finally, terminate the session distinctly to demarcate the hypnotic state from conscious awareness, preventing unintended naps and reinforcing the return to wakefulness.

Self-hypnosis unfolds as a powerful tool for cultivating tranquility amid life's chaos. Its practice holds the potential for substantial empowerment and inner peace.

1. Relaxation

Your initial task during the hypnotic induction is to ease into relaxation and calmness without attempting to forcefully coerce your mind into relaxation. Achieving profound relaxation—a skill many have not fully mastered—is essential but often overlooked. While some find it effortless to release tension, allowing each muscle to become supple and serene, others might struggle. If you belong to the former group, commence your self-hypnosis practice by embracing this relaxation method. It's crucial not to rush; take your time to achieve this state.

The duration required for the relaxation phase in self-hypnosis induction can vary widely, from as short as a few seconds to as long as half an hour. This phase is pivotal and shouldn't be underestimated. As your proficiency improves, you'll identify profoundly relaxed states and reach them surprisingly swiftly. However, as a novice, investing time in this phase is invaluable.

One prevalent method for achieving deep relaxation is the Jacobson Progressive Relaxation technique. It involves sequentially tensing and then releasing major muscle groups across your body, starting from the feet and lower legs, and moving upwards to the upper legs, hips, abdomen, and so forth. The process entails tensing each muscle group for a few seconds before consciously letting go.

2. Deepen

Once you've completed the relaxation phase in your self-hypnosis induction, the next step is to deepen the relaxed state. Transitioning into a hypnotic state can occur at any point between deep relaxation and the deepening procedures, though as a beginner, you might not immediately recognize it.

One initial challenge beginners encounter is the inclination to "watch for it," eagerly awaiting a change in awareness or sensation that signifies being in a hypnotic state. This anticipation can impede your progress. Entering a hypnotic state is akin to falling asleep—trying to pinpoint the precise moment you drift off to sleep often keeps you awake. Similarly, you won't be consciously aware of entering hypnosis, but you haven't lost consciousness.

With regular practice over a few weeks or months, you'll become more attuned to recognizing the hypnotic state within yourself. The time it takes to reach a profound hypnotic state varies widely among individuals. While some experience an extraordinary shift during their first attempt, others might practice for days without noticing substantial changes. Persistence is key; continued practice will eventually lead to success.

One of the most commonly used techniques for deepening the hypnotic state is the countdown method, frequently depicted in movies. To employ this technique, begin counting downward from a chosen number (such as 20 or 100) and adjust the count according to your comfort after a few practice sessions. Envision drifting into a deeper state with each count. During the count, random thoughts or images might intrude; acknowledge them and gently redirect your focus back to the count.

The pace of your countdown should feel natural—neither too swift nor too sluggish. For most people, a rate of about one count for every two or three seconds is comfortable. Some individuals synchronize their count with their breathing, slowing it down as they delve deeper. It's essential to conduct this count internally to minimize physical involvement and movement, aiming for a relaxed and effortless experience.

3. Apply Suggestion

Once you've completed the deepening phase, it's time to apply suggestions. Throughout the relaxation and deepening procedures, you've increased your suggestibility, opening your subconscious mind to receive these suggestions. The subconscious mind has distinctive and unique characteristics that make this process effective.

The most straightforward method to apply suggestions is by preparing and memorizing them in advance. These suggestions should be concise and personally composed, making them easier to recall. When ready, you can effortlessly guide yourself through these suggestions by simply thinking about them during this stage.

Conversing with yourself, essentially a monologue, is acceptable. Use the first-person personal pronoun "I" since you're directing these thoughts inwardly. Some suggestions can be brief and formal, like "I am eating less and becoming more slender every day." Others might be more detailed and free-flowing, such as "Food holds less importance in my life daily, and I fill my time with meaningful pursuits, making it easier to resist desserts and unhealthy foods..."

Typically, image suggestions, devoid of language, tend to be the most impactful. This involves picturing yourself in a serene and composed state amid a chaotic situation, visualizing this scenario in your mind's eye.

While some may notice immediate effects from their suggestions, it often takes time for them to take effect. Patience is essential; significant changes might not manifest right away. However, if after a couple of weeks, you don't perceive any results, consider altering your suggestions to better suit your needs and goals.

4. Termination

Upon completing the application of suggestions, your induction comes to an end, and it's time to terminate your session. Simply opening your eyes and moving on isn't recommended.

Formally signifying the conclusion of each session is crucial. This clear boundary distinguishes between the hypnotic state and your regular conscious awareness. A decisive termination also prevents your self-hypnosis practice from inadvertently transitioning into a nap. If a nap is desired, take it separately from self-hypnosis practice to avoid associating sleep with your sessions.

During bedtime practice, if you're indifferent about proceeding into sleep, it's acceptable. However, mentally establish the end of your self-hypnosis session.

To conclude the session, internally affirm that you will be fully awake and alert by counting up to, for instance, three.

"One, I'm beginning to transition to a waking state. Two, I'm becoming more alert and preparing to awaken. Three, I'm completely awake." Something along these lines.

Consistent practice of self-hypnosis can yield remarkable results in relaxation. It's personally one of the most rewarding practices I've ever adopted!

Now, let's transition to stress management techniques in general. These techniques are highly beneficial, though they could be extensive, but incredibly helpful.

CHAPTER 11

Stress Management

Stress is an inherent aspect of life. Surprisingly, some stress can serve as a positive motivator, pushing us beyond our usual boundaries and encouraging bold actions we might otherwise hesitate to take.

Building resilience is key to effectively managing stress. It involves mastering the art of harnessing stress to amplify rather than hinder our lives. Taking control of stress and transforming it into a force that works in your favor is crucial.

Detecting stress symptoms serves as a call to action. Swift recognition often leads to proactive steps. While it's not always evident why stress occurs in each circumstance, common events like the loss of a loved one, the birth of a child, career advancements, or new relationships can trigger stress as we readjust our lives.

Your body signals the need for assistance when stress symptoms arise. In this chapter, numerous suggestions will be provided. Not all may resonate with you, but we believe some will indeed prove helpful.

Stress management primarily revolves around three major approaches.

The action-oriented approach involves identifying stress-inducing issues and implementing necessary changes for a more stress-free life.

Emotionally oriented approaches entail viewing the stressful situation from a different perspective, often with humor or altered perceptions, which can defuse its impact.

I particularly advocate for this approach. Sometimes, laughing at a situation prevents uncontrollable tears. It's about seeing the humor amid potential doom.

The acceptance-oriented approach centers on surviving stress linked to past problems.

To begin managing stress effectively, start by understanding its root cause. No one comprehends your problem better than you. Spend a few moments assessing your true feelings; it can alter the entire situation.

Identify the trigger that led to stress. If someone close is nearby, consider confiding in them. When overwhelmed, taking deep breaths and counting to ten can infuse your system with extra oxygen and rejuvenate your body.

During severe stress, pause, meditate for a moment, and momentarily detach from the situation. Stand up, walk, and stretch; you'll soon feel the stress dissipating. Relaxation serves as the finest antidote to stress.

Smiling is a simple yet effective stress management tool. A mere smile directed at a colleague across the room at work can significantly alter your mood. Learn basic yoga or meditation techniques; these practices work wonders.

Feel free to devise your personalized stress management techniques. The essence lies in identifying the stress cause, briefly disengaging from it, and then addressing it. Taking a brief walk or observing nature can alleviate stress. Drinking water, playing simple games, or altering your focus of attention often diminishes the perceived enormity of the problem when you return to it.

Here are five quick steps that can effectively alleviate stress:

1. **Get Moving**: Motion creates emotion. When idle, it's easier to feel low. Take a challenge now; regardless of your mood, get up and move around briskly. Even jumping in an empty room for a few minutes works like magic.

Exercise is a fantastic stress buster, though it might worry those with anxiety disorders. Remind yourself there's a difference between physical exercise and a panic attack.

2. **Embrace New Experiences**: Invest in that dream trip you've been longing for. Explore exotic places to stimulate your imagination and creativity. Detach from your routine and take a leap into something novel.

3. **Aid Others:** Helping others is therapeutic. Dive into supporting others facing challenges. However, avoid getting entangled in their issues. Recognize your boundaries and know when to step back to reassess your own priorities.

4. **Find Humor:** Laughter is an excellent stress reliever. It eases tension, increases blood flow, and releases chemicals that alleviate pain. Embrace laughter by visiting comedy clubs or watching funny movies.

5. **Find Solace:** Prayer or meditation serves as a sustainable remedy during tough times. Regardless of faith, having a place to find peace and center yourself is invaluable.

CHAPTER 12

Long-Term Stress Management

Here are 13 effective stress management tips aimed at regaining calm and peace in the long run:

1. **Embrace Stress:** Understand that stress can be beneficial. Harness its energy to boost performance when required. Recognize its role in pushing you forward, much like top athletes perform better with a certain level of stress.
2. **Avoid Negative Influences**: Negative individuals can be stress triggers. Limit contact with them and be cautious about being drawn into their negativity. While helping them manage stress is commendable, prioritize your own well-being.
3. **Learn from Good Managers:** Observe and emulate those who handle stress well. Analyze their attitude, behavior,

and strategies. Engage in conversations with them to understand their approach to stress management.

4. **Practice Deep Breathing:** Use deep breathing to induce relaxation. Inhale slowly for a count of 7 and exhale for a count of 11. Repeat until your heart rate steadies and you feel calmer.

5. **Halt Stressful Thoughts:** Interrupt spiraling stress thoughts by challenging their likelihood of occurrence. Redirect your focus on preventive actions rather than worrying needlessly.

6. **Identify Stress Triggers**: Identify specific situations or circumstances that trigger stress. Understanding these triggers empowers you to take action to minimize their impact.

7. **Prioritize Health:** Adequate sleep, proper diet, and exercise are essential for stress management. Avoid using substances like alcohol, nicotine, or caffeine as stress relievers.

8. **Connect with Nature:** Spending time outdoors, soaking in sunlight, and engaging in activities can significantly reduce stress levels, leading to a more positive outlook on life.

9. **Embrace Playfulness:** Revisit activities you enjoyed as a child. Engage in creative or playful endeavors without worrying about societal expectations.

10. **Set Realistic Goals:** Avoid setting unattainable goals to prevent feelings of failure. Allow sufficient time and understand that occasional setbacks are part of the journey.

11. **Learn to Say 'No'**: Understand the importance of setting boundaries. It's okay to decline or say 'no' when necessary to prioritize personal well-being.

12. **Prioritize Self-Care:** Meeting your own needs allows you to support others effectively without compromising your happiness.

13. **Make Time for Yourself:** Prioritize your well-being to find more fulfillment in assisting others without feeling compelled to sacrifice your needs consistently.

CHAPTER 13

Integrating Self-Care with Stress Management

Here are 9 additional ways to integrate self-care with stress management, to relax and de-stress:

1. **Yell:** Let out a guttural yelp or scream in a private space like your car to release pent-up tension and emotions.
2. **Sing**: Belt out a favorite song, regardless of your singing abilities, as a way to release stress and uplift your mood.
3. **Explore a New Hobby:** Engage in activities like knitting, crocheting, or any craft that promotes relaxation through repetitive motions and allows time for contemplation.
4. **Start a Garden**: Cultivate plants, flowers, or a small garden space, even in pots, to experience the therapeutic benefits of tending to and watching things grow.

5. **Play with Pets:** Interacting with animals, like dogs or cats, can alleviate stress and offer companionship without the pressure of social expectations.
6. **Stargaze:** Lie down, observe the night sky, and contemplate its vastness to gain perspective and find solace in the beauty and scale of the universe.
7. **Enjoy Comfort Food:** Indulge in your favorite comforting dishes in moderation to evoke a sense of ease and relaxation.
8. **Swing**: Experience the carefree feeling of swinging, whether at a playground or by installing a swing in your yard, to rediscover a liberating sensation.
9. **Take a Candlelit Bubble Bath:** Create a tranquil environment by bathing in warm water with candlelight, allowing stress to melt away.

Finding activities that alleviate stress and practicing them regularly is crucial to maintaining overall well-being. The key is to discover what works best for you and integrate it into your routine.

CHAPTER 14

Being Able to Say No

A significant challenge faced by many individuals over-whelmed with stress is the struggle to say "No" when necessary. This tendency often arises from a people-pleasing disposition, where putting others' needs before one's own becomes a habit-ual response. While being considerate isn't inherently negative, incessant people-pleasing can be a significant stressor.

People pleasers habitually prioritize others' needs, often at the expense of their own well-being. They hesitate to express their thoughts or desires and refrain from asking for what they need. This perpetual concern for others can be exhausting, leaving them feeling anxious, drained, and frequently unappreciated.

As someone who fell into this trap, I understand the constant agreement to help others while feeling a void when needing similar support. People pleasers often believe that asking for help obligates others, assuming they should volunteer without being prompted.

This inclination arises from an upbringing where their needs were overlooked or were expected to tend to others' requirements. In various cultures, girls and those identifying closely with their mothers are particularly conditioned to prioritize others' needs over their own.

The relentless focus on others often leaves people pleasers feeling emotionally disconnected from themselves. Yet, it's possible to alter this pattern and regain a sense of self-worth.

Breaking free from this cycle requires practicing the art of saying "No." It's crucial to start small and gradually build confidence. Consider responses like, "I need to think about it" or "Let me check my schedule and get back to you" before automatically saying "Yes."

Embrace small breaks without guilt, as prioritizing mental health is crucial. Discover activities that bring personal joy and allow yourself to indulge in them without remorse. Additionally, learn to ask for help when needed – it's a mutual exchange.

Self-awareness is key; being mindful of your feelings and thoughts is a fundamental aspect of reclaiming your identity. Expressing yourself genuinely is vital, though tact should be exercised in certain situations.

Remember, genuine connections are not based solely on doing things for others. Taking care of oneself, saying "No," and carving out personal time is essential for mental well-being. Your journey toward change begins with these small, intentional steps.

CHAPTER 15

Balancing Work and Self-Care

Often, we're aware deep down that we need a break. Whether it's a full-fledged vacation or a simple weekend getaway, stepping away from the daily grind can be incredibly rejuvenating and an effective way to alleviate stress and anxiety.

Sadly, many of us believe we can't spare the time to get away. This toxic thinking perpetuates a cycle of overworking ourselves, compromising our productivity and well-being.

Think about those moments when you kept working, knowing your attention wasn't fully on the task. The mind wanders, words blur, and the same sentence gets rewritten repeatedly. Perhaps you've longed for a break from family or responsibilities but hesitated due to anticipated consequences. It's time for that break.

Why do we resist taking timeouts? There are genuine reasons to complete tasks, yet sometimes, hidden agendas hinder us. It could be ego-driven, seeking validation by boasting about work hours or effort invested in projects.

Perhaps you feel you can't take time off. "I must finish this now" becomes a never-ending loop, moving from one task to the next, never stopping. Feeling indispensable might drive you to avoid breaks, fearing the system will crumble without your constant effort.

Others feel they need to be needed. Mothers managing households fear their absence would cause chaos. Yet, this conviction isn't reason enough to deny oneself rest.

Break free from such thoughts! Taking time for yourself yields incredible benefits. Allowing your mind and body to rest sharpens focus, boosts motivation, relieves stress, and aids muscle recovery. Athletes stress the importance of rest in training; similarly, your brain, a muscle in its own right, needs rest to perform optimally.

Deciding to take a break is commendable! It can be a short meditation or a world trip, anything that diverts your mind from the everyday monotony.

Depending on the time available, enjoy activities like reading, movies, cooking, spending time with loved ones, exercising, or traveling. During this break, permit yourself this time without guilt. You'll gain immensely from this self-care.

Despite your thoughts, life continues without you, and everyone survives even when you're not there. Let go of everything and focus on yourself for once, instead of everyone around you.

Feeling tired or unmotivated shouldn't be viewed negatively. Taking a break can significantly enhance efficiency and effectiveness in every aspect of life. Consider it a much-needed recharge for your deserving self.

You might assume these techniques won't work around colleagues. But you'd be mistaken.

CHAPTER 16

Relaxation Techniques

Amidst the hustle and bustle of work, finding moments to relax is essential. Contrary to popular belief, frequent coffee or smoke breaks might add to the stress experienced during the workday. Yet, there exists a tried-and-tested method to relax, right at your desk.

Firstly, secure a comfortable sitting position. Maintain an upright posture, with your back against the chair, feet flat on the ground, and hands gently resting on your thighs. If plausible, close your eyes; while optional, this simple act can amplify relaxation.

Commence a rhythmic breathing exercise. Inhale slowly through your nostrils, counting silently to 5. Hold your breath for a count of 5. Exhale gradually, also counting to 5. Repeat this pattern.

This exercise involves a sequence of tensing and releasing specific muscle groups. When tensing, exert pressure without causing discomfort. Upon release, aim for complete relaxation.

Start by tensing your feet, pulling them upward while keeping the heels grounded. Hold for 5 and then let go, feeling the ensuing relaxation. Then, tense your thigh muscles, hold, and release. Follow this with the abdomen, then the muscles in your arms and hands, squeezing them into fists. Release and relish the relaxation.

Continue with the upper back, pushing the shoulders back as if uniting the shoulder blades. Next, raise your shoulders toward your ears as if shrugging, hold, and then relax. Proceed to the neck, gently tilting your head back and then forward, releasing any tension.

Shift to your facial muscles, opening your mouth wide, raising your eyebrows, and tightly closing your eyes. Hold each for 5 counts and then relax, allowing your face to ease into a state of calmness.

Conclude the exercise with breathing cycles—inhaling, holding, and exhaling, each for a count of 5. Repeat this sequence four times.

Practice this relaxation technique whenever needed, except when driving, to alleviate tension. Over time, this exercise will enable you to identify and relax tense muscles instantly. For prolonged benefits, perform at least twice daily.

Customize and expand this routine by targeting specific tension-prone areas. Pair this exercise with visualization—imagine a serene place for at least 5 minutes, transporting yourself to a peaceful mental oasis.

CHAPTER 17

Conclusion

If there's one thing you take away from this book, let it be this: stress cannot be entirely eliminated from our lives. However, what you can do is learn how to channel stress in a way that benefits you.

Managing stress doesn't have to be an overwhelming task. But we can't stress this enough: if you're feeling excessively stressed, seeking guidance from a healthcare professional, spiritual advisor or mental health organization can be incredibly beneficial. Stress reactions might contribute to disorders like depression or anxiety, so consulting with a psychiatrist, psychologist, or counselor might offer valuable support.

Our aim is not to pose as medical experts. We simply strive to equip you with tools that can assist you in dealing with overwhelming situations that make you feel out of control.

Considering time management tools might also alleviate some of your stress. Feeling pressed for time can compound stress and potentially lead to anxiety, which isn't something you want to experience.

Practicing stress management techniques is cost-effective and straightforward. They can be implemented almost anywhere and at any time, offering immediate relief. If you feel overwhelmed, seeking help should not be delayed. Sometimes, the cause of stress might not be apparent or might have physical roots, and seeking assistance from others might provide a solution.

Stress is a natural aspect of life. In small amounts, it can be beneficial, motivating increased productivity. However, excessive stress or an intense response to stress can be detrimental, leading to various health issues like infection, heart disease, or depression. Persistent stress often triggers anxiety and unhealthy coping behaviors such as overeating or substance abuse.

While the causes of stress vary from person to person, finding healthy lifestyle adjustments and enjoyable coping strategies tends to help most individuals. I hope the strategies provided in this book will assist you in dealing with the stress we all encounter!

Remember, you're not alone in this struggle. Countless individuals grapple with feeling overwhelmed and out of control. This book aims to guide you toward inner peace, reminding you that we're all part of this vast world for a purpose.

Embrace life fully, and when stress hits or panic looms, take a moment to relax, breathe deeply, and acknowledge that many others can empathize with your feelings.